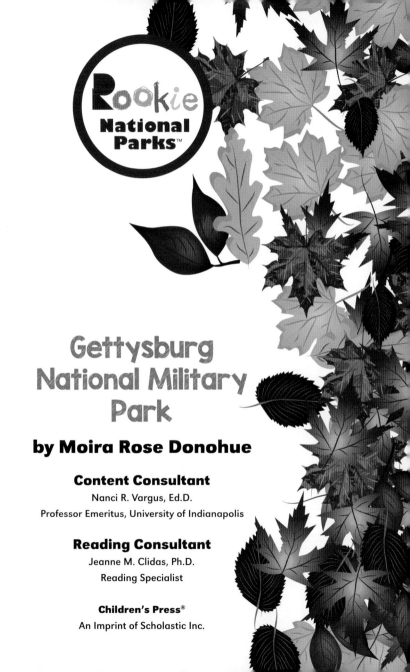

Gettysburg National Military Park

by Moira Rose Donohue

Content Consultant

Nanci R. Vargus, Ed.D.
Professor Emeritus, University of Indianapolis

Reading Consultant

Jeanne M. Clidas, Ph.D.
Reading Specialist

Children's Press®
An Imprint of Scholastic Inc.

Library of Congress Cataloging-in-Publication Data
Names: Donohue, Moira Rose, author.
Title: Gettysburg National Military Park/by Moira Rose Donohue.
Description: New York, NY: Children's Press, an Imprint of Scholastic Inc., 2019. |
Series: Rookie National Parks | Includes index.
Identifiers: LCCN 2018023402| ISBN 9780531133194 (library binding) |
ISBN 9780531137222 (pbk.)
Subjects: LCSH: Gettysburg National Military Park (Pa.)—Juvenile literature. |
Gettysburg, Battle of, Gettysburg, Pa., 1863—Juvenile literature.
Classification: LCC E475.56 .D66 2019 | DDC 974.8/42—dc23

Produced by Spooky Cheetah Press
Design: Ed LoPresti Graphic Design
Creative Direction: Judith E. Christ for Scholastic Inc.

Published in 2019 by Children's Press, an imprint of Scholastic Inc.

Printed in Heshan, China 62

SCHOLASTIC, CHILDREN'S PRESS, ROOKIE NATIONAL PARKS™, and
associated logos are trademarks and/or registered trademarks of Scholastic Inc.

1 2 3 4 5 6 7 8 9 10 R 28 27 26 25 24 23 22 21 20 19

Scholastic, Inc., 557 Broadway, New York, NY 10012.

Photos ©: cover: DelmasLehman/iStockphoto; back cover: Craig Fildes/Getty Images; "Ranger
Red Fox" by Bill Mayer for Scholastic; 1-2: Cleo Design/Shutterstock; 3: Tetra Images/Robert
Harding Picture Library; 4-5: Loop Images/UIG/Getty Images; 6-7: Christopher L. Smith/age
fotostock; 8-9: Ilene MacDonald/Alamy Images; 10-11: TIM SLOAN/AFP/Getty Images; 12-13
background: Vespasian/Alamy Images; 13 inset: Joe Raedle/Getty Images; 14-15 background:
littleny/iStockphoto; 15 inset: Jon Bilous/Shutterstock; 16-17 background: Chronicle/Alamy
Images; 16 inset: Dennis Cox/Alamy Images; 18-19: Maxlevoyou/iStockphoto; 20: Glenn
Bartley/BIA/Minden Pictures; 21: rewindtime/iStockphoto; 22-23 background: TIM SLOAN/AFP/
Getty Images; 23 inset: Jeff Mcdougal/EyeEm/Getty Images; 24-25: Cannons fire at Gettysburg
Battlefield 150th Anniversary (photo)/Greg Dale/National Geographic Creative/Bridgeman
Images; 26 left: Morey Milbradt/Alamy Images; 26 center: Wim Wiskerke/Alamy Images; 26
right: Franck Fotos/Alamy Images; 27 left: Kristi Blokhin/Shutterstock; 27 center: Ben Spires/
Alamy Images; 27 right: James Brunker/Alamy Images; 30 top: Maurice Savage/Alamy Images;
30 center top: Zack Frank/Shutterstock; 30 center bottom: Rainer Grosskopf/Getty Images; 30
bottom: Felix Lipov/Shutterstock; 31 top: Weird NJ/Splash News/Newscom; 31 bottom: Everett
Historical/Shutterstock; 31 center top: Vespasian/Alamy Images; 32: Tetra Images/Robert
Harding Picture Library.

Maps by Jim McMahon/Mapman ®.

Table of Contents

I am Ranger Red Fox, your tour guide. Are you ready for an amazing adventure at Gettysburg?

Troops from 30 states fought at Gettysburg. Monuments around the park, such as this one for Ohio, honor each state.

Welcome to Gettysburg National Military Park!

Gettysburg is in Pennsylvania. A big battle took place there from July 1 to July 3, 1863. The battle was the deadliest ever fought in the United States. About 50,000 soldiers were wounded or died.

In 1895, the battlefield was made a national **military** park.

United States

Pennsylvania →
Gettysburg
National
Military Park

N
W ◆ E
S

Lincoln's Gettysburg
Address Monument

Gettysburg is also famous because President Abraham Lincoln gave an important speech there. It is known as the Gettysburg Address. Lincoln said that the world should "never forget" why the soldiers died.

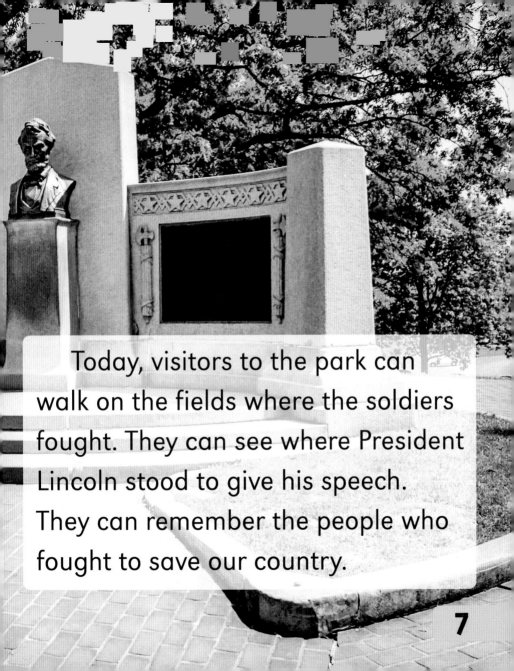

Today, visitors to the park can walk on the fields where the soldiers fought. They can see where President Lincoln stood to give his speech. They can remember the people who fought to save our country.

The Friend to Friend monument remembers how friends fought on opposite sides of the war.

Union soldiers wore blue uniforms and Confederates wore gray.

Chapter 1

Friend vs. Friend

The Battle of Gettysburg was part of the American Civil War (1861–1865). A civil war is a fight between people in the same country.

The war was fought between the North and the South. The North was called the Union. The South was the Confederacy.

More than 600,000 people died in the Civil War.

Slavery was an issue that divided the nation. Soon after President Lincoln was elected, states in the South **seceded** from the United States. War broke out on April 12, 1861.

After two years of fighting, the armies met outside the town of Gettysburg. A giant 360-degree painting at the park's Visitor Center shows a scene from the battle.

These ridges are rows of rocky hills that formed more than 180 million years ago!

Chapter 2

Three-Day Battle

On the first day of the battle, the Confederates pushed the Union army to the top of Cemetery **Ridge**. Across a large field they could see another ridge facing them. The Confederate army lined up there. It was Seminary Ridge.

Park visitors see the same flowers soldiers saw.

Today, visitors can climb among the boulders in Devil's Den.

DEVIL'S DEN

Some Union soldiers scrambled into Devil's Den to hide. That's a cluster of rough and uneven granite rocks at the end of Cemetery Ridge. But soon they were pushed out by Confederate soldiers.

On day two, the Confederate soldiers tried to capture a nearby hill called Little Round Top. But brave Union soldiers surprised them and beat them to the top.

This monument sits on Little Round Top and honors New York troops.

On the third day of fighting, Confederate General George Pickett charged across the field. Visitors to this spot can imagine him and his men racing

The park has more than 400 cannons, like this one.

across the open field trying to dodge Union bullets and cannonballs. Nearly all of Pickett's men died. The Union ultimately won the Battle of Gettysburg. It was the turning point in the war.

Union soldiers held off Pickett's Charge.

Chapter 3

Never Forget

About 3,500 Union soldiers are buried at Gettysburg. On November 19, 1863, President Lincoln gave his address at the cemetery. Two years later, the war was over. The country was again united and slavery was no longer allowed.

Today, people can visit the cemetery. They can imagine hearing Lincoln's famous words.

Some of the oak trees in the park are the same ones that were there during the battle. They are called witness trees. How do historians know the trees were alive then? Many have holes from the bullets.

Visitors might also see a bird like the black-throated blue warbler hidden in one of these trees. The soldiers might have seen— and heard— these birds, too!

black-throated blue warbler

At least a dozen witness trees, like this one, can be found in the park.

witness tree at Devil's Den

The park covers about 6,000 acres. That's the size of 6,000 football fields!

Chapter 4

Touring History

Millions of people travel to Gettysburg each year. Visitors can watch a movie about the battle at the Museum and Visitor Center. Then they can tour the park in their cars, on foot, on bicycles, or even on Segways! Some visitors take a tour on horseback.

The Pennsylvania monument is the largest in the park.

In spring and summer, park rangers give living history demonstrations. They even fire some of the old Civil War cannons.

These men, dressed as Union soldiers, honor the 150th anniversary of the battle.

Today, soldiers from many wars are buried in the cemetery at Gettysburg. The park is a place to learn. It is a place to remember.

Imagine you could visit Gettysburg National Military Park. What would you do there?

These are some of the monuments, memorials, and markers in the Gettysburg National Military Park.

High Water Mark of the Rebellion marks the farthest point reached by the Confederates

Eternal Light Peace Memorial honored veterans on the 75th anniversary of the battle

Women's Memorial recognizes the women who helped and suffered during the battle

Monuments by the Numbers
The park is home to about...

1,320 monuments and markers

4 memorials to individuals

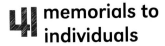

Be a good visitor and don't climb on the cannons or monuments!

Lincoln's Gettysburg Address Monument honors Lincoln's address, which was given a short distance away from the monument

Soldiers' National Monument stands for peace and freedom

First Shot Marker marks where the first shot was fired by Union army soldier Marcellus Jones

12 Confederate state memorials

18 Union state memorials

Oh no! Ranger Red Fox has lost his way in the park. But you can help. Use the map and the clues below to find him.

1. Ranger Red Fox hiked up Seminary Ridge, where the Confederate army gathered at the Battle of Gettysburg.

2. After a nap, he trotted south across the field to Devil's Den and climbed the granite rocks.

3. Then he raced east and scrambled up Little Round Top.

4. Finally he trudged north and stood on top of the ridge where the Union army stood.

Help!
Can you
find me?

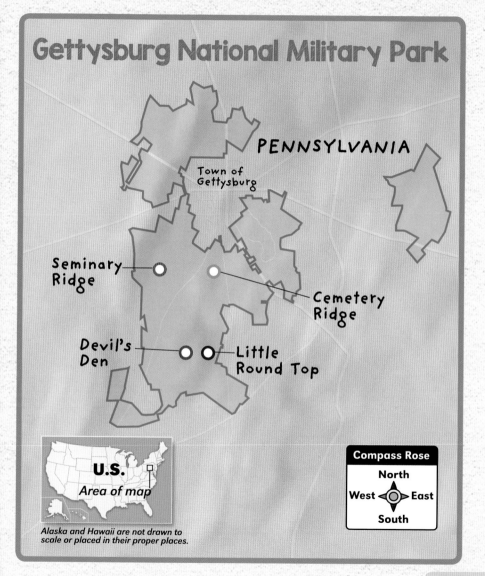

Gettysburg National Military Park

PENNSYLVANIA

Town of Gettysburg

Seminary Ridge

Cemetery Ridge

Devil's Den

Little Round Top

U.S.
Area of map

Alaska and Hawaii are not drawn to scale or placed in their proper places.

Compass Rose

North

West — East

South

Learn About the Generals

Gettysburg has many monuments that honor the generals who fought there. If you visit the park, try to find them!

General Robert E. Lee
Lee was the leader of the Confederate forces. His statue is on top of the tall Virginia monument.

General George Meade
Meade led the Union forces. He's shown on his horse, Old Baldy.

General Gouverneur Warren
Warren's statue stands on Little Round Top, the Union position he saved.

General James Longstreet
Longstreet's statue shows the Confederate general, who ordered Pickett's Charge, riding into battle.

Glossary

military (**mil**-i-ter-ee): of or having to do with soldiers, the armed forces, or war

ridge (**rij**): long, narrow chain of mountains or hills

seceded (si-**see**-ded): formally withdrew from the United States

slavery (**slay**-vur-ee): a condition in which some people own other people as property

Index

Facts for Now

Visit this Scholastic Web site for more information
on Gettysburg National Military Park:
www.factsfornow.scholastic.com
Enter the keyword **Gettysburg**

About the Author

Moira Rose Donohue has written over 25 books for children. She loves history and animals and has visited many national parks. On her second visit to Gettysburg, she made sure to visit Little Round Top. Moira lives in Florida with her dog, Petunia.